# More Daring Escapes

# More Daring Escapes

*Poems*

❦

## Steven Huff

*For Len*
*with thanks*
*and in*
*appreciation for*
*your work*
*Steven Huff*
*11/9/07*

🐓 RED HEN PRESS | *Los Angeles, California*

More Daring Escapes

Copyright © 2008 by Steven Huff

Book design by Mark E. Cull

ISBN: 978-1-59709-079-7
Library of Congress Catalog Card Number: 2007936716

The City of Los Angeles Department of Cultural Affairs, Los Angeles County Arts Commission, California Arts Council and the National Endowment for the Arts partially support Red Hen Press.

Published by Red Hen Press
www.redhen.org

ACKNOWLEDGEMENTS

Grateful acknowledgment is made to the editors of the following journals and anthologies where some of the poems in this book, or earlier versions of them, first appeared:

"Mirrors," and "With Some Poets in Baltimore, 2003," in *The Carlton Review*; "Second Coming in Northern Pennsylvania," in *Commonwealth: Contemporary Poets on Pennsylvania*, edited by Marjorie Maddox and Jerry Wemple, University of Pennsylvania Press 2005; "Jet Lag," in *The Marlboro Review*; "The First Time I Heard Elvis," in *Never Before: Poems about First Experiences*, edited by Laure-Anne Bosselaar, Four-Way Books, 2005; "Future Farmers," in *Ploughshares*; "Small Gestures" in *Redactions*; "Boarding the Bus," and "That Was When We Got Lost, After the Movie," in *Tar River Poetry*; "Dream, No Dream," "Remembering Tony while Awaiting My Own Biopsy Results," and "All Those Houses," in *Two Rivers Review*; "A Bestiary of Continuous Extinctions," in *The Dire Elegies*, Karla Linn Merrifield and Roger Wier, editors, FootHills Publishing, 2006; "Boarding a Bus," "Dream, No Dream," "Remembering Tony while Awaiting My Own Biopsy Results," "Deliverance," "Daring to Call New York" (as "First Call to New York"), "For My 19,723rd Day," "A Likely Story, Actaeon," "One Thing's for Sure," "That Was when We Got Lost, after the Movie," "Nothing Holds up Like Your Bones," and "Left on the Road in the Nevada Desert" were included in *Proof*, a chapbook published by *Two Rivers Review*, and which was named Editor's Choice in the magazine's 2004 Chapbook Competition, Phil Memmer, editor.

This Book is for Betsy

# Contents

One

# Without Trumpets

## Second Coming in Northern Pennsylvania

I'm driving back into the woods, deep into the mountains
        that once gave me away
like an unadmired bride, driving out of New York
        into Bradford, PA and on into

Custer City where people may still share my genes but look
        at me suspiciously over their cups,
driving deep, deep, like another of my deeds done
        in haste in a back seat

on a road with no lights, deep, still seeking those old angels
        that drank from the oil creeks.
I don't even know who's the governor here now,
        much less my blood ones

who turned their dark backs and went into the past,
        big and serious as boulders
though they remain in my eyes, or deep into woods vast
        enough to hide from me for eons,

who convinced me young that Jesus would come before I'd ever
        grow up, drive a car,
love and marry, and go to hell broke. But He didn't come,
        and now it's me coming back,

alone, old folks, old ghosts, on bald tires. Coming
        without trumpets. It's me.

## Dream, No Dream

*Hara: the central abdomen, the body-mind center*

She dreamed she saw her mother and father walking into the woods
holding hands and she couldn't catch them. Later she dreamed she rode
to their double funeral and her dog was driving. Ever more absurd,
she saw them laid out in caskets in their old wedding clothes.
So, what are dreams for? she asked me. I said, Maybe they're
our natural koens. Maybe the heart asks the brain, Who am I?
Or the brain asks the hara. And thus you get a dumbfounding dream
for reply, and you don't even know it contains the answer.

I wanted to marry her, but it wasn't to be. Although I dreamed as vividly
as she: We dragged a Christmas tree on foot from Mohonk to the city
over hills till hell would have been easier. She was both my wives
and also herself, as happens in dreams, and we *had* to have a tree.
Once I found her apartment house in a dense fog, and we had wine
and seven minutes before she and her husband had to go out—
so I went back out to the fog, a little flushed.
What are you dreaming now, love? the heart asks the hara.
And the hara answers, Where is the heart?
The head answers, There is no heart. Life is a dream, but there is no dream.

*When I Have Money*

I'm going to take a handful to town
and stock up
on razorblades, mouthwash, toilet
paper, wine and oatmeal.

On those nights when I wake
and see eternity right through the ceiling,
I won't feel so naked—
when I have money, and razors.

And I'd fight a bear
to protect my oatmeal, my marmalade,
instead of inviting him in
to see for himself.

And while making love I won't
suddenly yell, There's no coffee!

## All Those Houses I Built

are still empty. No one moved
into the Greek revival
at the edge of town; empty still
is the neo-villa I built in the poplars
with my bloody knuckles;
the ranch house I raised
hammer over saw is dark
as a vow of abstinence.
Flaccid power lines
and juiceless meters, that's what
I've got. No man, no woman
cooks risotto in the two-storey lake front,
nor undresses in the curtainless
bungalow on Mulberry Road.

All the sweet lingerie I dreamed
in those drawers
when I snapped that chalk line
across the under-floor of the duplex,
the barrels of party-garbage my
mind's eye carted to the curb
in front of the Dutch colonial,
some grumbling papa in his
underwear twisting
the thermostat like a child's ear
in the cedar A-frame,
or Shake 'n' Bake and baby-bedlam
in the Cape Cod— *all that*
I bequeathed with every miter joint,
every screw in a hole, every

nail driven home.
I did the work of creation.
So now, what's the matter with everyone?

## Going Home to the Farm via Hypnotic Age-Regression

I can't stay long, hypnotism isn't cheap.
I only came to say, Relax,
Russia will never drop the bomb.

We turn a shovel of soil by the milk house: worms
and blue stones mean eternity
(I realize that now), which was with us all along—

joke's on us. But stupid, I've searched
the earth for meaning anyway.
What else can I tell you that would do any good?

Oh, the god-picture we framed and hung in the old house?
Yeah, that was really him. He
showed himself from a cloud in 1999,

and we all fell on our faces. And the god
in the woods, in the rock-covered well?
Sure, why not? God in the hay, in the hornets' nest,

god in the busted fridge in the barn
with our trunks of old clothes
in which we were once in fashion? Yes.

But, damn all that. Take me to see the chickens.

## The DeSoto

We needed a farm truck, so we made one out of the '51 DeSoto,
cut its ass-end off with a hacksaw, right across the roof
behind the front seat (threw the old
back seat in the barn), unbolted,
broke welds, and stripped down the rear chassis
so it looked scared and trouserless. Then we built a wooden
flatbed on that spindly frame. Needless to say, it
wasn't much of a truck, too light: six, eight bales
and the bed rubbed the rear tires. Once we
bolted a plywood snow-scoop to
the front bumper, wrapped the treads with
chains, but it just sat there spinning
on ice. Piece of shit. But we all learned to
drive in it, we kids. At night if you wanted to
sleep and dream by the creek, you drove it
over the hill, no lights, no muffler,
rumbling like a rhino with an intestinal disorder, fast and dark,
with de Soto himself glaring from the hood.

*Attica*


My town was famous for its prison, for its dead and how they died,
and for the ones my town blamed: those jailhouse rioters
        in their terrifying hoods.

But I had a life there. Whistled out of the foundry every daybreak,
I wrung beer out of my paycheck, slept and rose with the ticking moon,
        back to the foundry,
hunkering from shadow to fire and back to shadow.

I once found a wide-eyed doll half sunk in shale by a rust-red creek.
Found a stairway behind a stairway. A bayonet stuck
        in a barn wall for hanging a bridle.

But what I wanted was goldfish, a great florescent tank in my house,
so when I'd come home dark and pissed off, or when
        I'd get up from bed
to sit alone, wakened by that hysterical whistle the prison blew
        every noon,

there'd be my enshrinement of fish, golden, in luminous gurgles.
        I know it makes no particular sense.

## Small Gestures

My father taught me small gestures
like pointing my thumb over
    my shoulder.
Do you think that's insignificant?
    Just cut off
your thumbs and try telling us where
    you've been,
or warning us not to go there.
    Or try being
president and blaming the excesses
    of a past
    administration
without benefit of a thumb over your
    shoulder.
Try being Jesus and saying, *Get thee
    behind me, Satan.*
    Do you see?
I learned what the big guys know.
And he taught me to roll up my sleeves.

## Jet-Lag

1. *Home from a midnight flight*

relighting my rooms,
red-eyed sorting of mail.
The furnace labors in *vox ursa*
to reheat the house.
Cats venture growling
from behind the couch.

2. *Last flight from Seattle*

an old Chinese couple next to me,
fondling and kissing
in the black sky.

Torches of the anonymous below.

3. *Airport shuttle back*

to my car, buried in snow.
Bashô still lies open
on my seat where I left him
nights ago, wandering north.

4. *I never knew*

until this house under
a landing path—
planes so low I can
read their numbers—

that the sky rolls and breaks behind
a plane like the wake of a boat.

Listen. And remember the brandy
you saved for solitary returns.

## A Bestiary of Continuous Extinctions

Something ended a moment ago, another species I didn't know existed.
Maybe it'll make the news: a bug, a bird, gone. I've grown too used

to this. There goes another now, blinking into oblivion like a light
turning itself inside out, into black. You, desert sloth, who drank

the rare berries of dew from sand flowers, you're gone—I didn't
know you. You, beetle with a conch-like shell, who burrowed into

spindly eucalyptus roots, we were never introduced. Luminous
two-horned tree frog. Orange-beekéd spotty woodpecker, starved

since the chestnuts bowed out of the forest, do I know you? Who
saw you off into the dark, little Siamese mantis? Where have I seen you,

Nigerian recluse bat? Nowhere, I'll bet. You didn't know me either;
is that more trouble? Does that mean I'm going with you now, ten-

wingéd Mongolian flying spider, through that poisoned door I've
helped to open, onto that silent ark? Are you taking me with you, blue-

indigo goatfly? Where are we going, ruby-tuskéd Madagascar boar?

## Remembering Tony While Awaiting My Own Biopsy Results

I told Tony we'd celebrate his new book next year.
And he said, *Hold that thought*. But I really knew better.
I could almost foresee his daughters, singing as they
washed his brittle corpse with sponges and soap,
turning the lamps golden-low in his cabin. I've known him long,
since his bleak apartment on Ellis Place. But while I wait for a train
on a winter night in Far Rockaway, I try not to think
of him—*I do think of him*. Doctors are somewhere examining
my own suspicious tissue like Queequeg mixing ashes in a gourd.
They're going to call me soon, somewhere, as if from a cloud.

The passengers on the platform are huddled,
their anonymity loud under their scarves. When you don't
know the trains, when you talk to no one, you chance ending up
where you never imagined. I think of Tony on a night train
in Mongolia, a strange boy asleep beside him pissing his pants.
Death was still many stops away. Now a train with no number
halts on the opposite track: I watch the bundled riders get off
and walk toward the dark, each body enveloped in its own vapor.

*—for Anthony Piccione 1939–2001*

## The First Time I Heard Elvis

Dad was on the tractor up ahead. Danny & Gary
& Billy & I were crammed in the truck cab behind,
chaff down our backs. Billy & I had been fooling
around the week before & set fire to a hay stack
& damn near caught the barn. We'd served our time
locked in our rooms pacing & listening to
little Linda singing in the yard below, making
us nuts, & we'd just got to the point where our crime
didn't come up in conversation every few minutes.
Truck radio suddenly played we were nothing but
hound dogs. Meaning everybody, I guess.

Classic case of kids with matches.  Danny & Gary knew
better—no sense crying all the time. But listen, now
*listen* to this guy, what's his name, Preston or
something? Billy scratching chaff down his back,
looking at Dad up ahead on the Deere who couldn't hear
this loose-lipped tune, the first I knew Dad not to
hear something. What was that name, Melvis?

They thought Billy & I were a couple of alarming
weeds, dangerous as smallpox. I'm not saying it was good,
what we did. But against all the bad clouds ahead of us,
the uncaught rabbits, & Gary going off
for a life on the road, that fire didn't mean beans.
Eventually Billy went to jail & little Linda to college,
like you'd expect. If you expect things. Like, that a
hound-dog will come when he's called, not guessing
he's about to get run down. Not high class. No sir.
A song like that makes you think.

Two

# Crazy

## A Woman You Saw at Mt. Vernon, in 1962

pushed an empty baby buggy
through the turn-style,
and walked like an ordinary tourist
in the stillness of the great father's house.

Later she parked it outside
and sat on the grass, and calmly
unwrapped a sandwich.
When you asked your mother
(it was a family trip, and she'd
noticed her too), *Do you think
she's crazy?* she nodded solemnly.

And that was all, you see:
a crazy woman with an empty baby buggy,
experiencing hunger
like an ordinary tourist,
took her sips of coffee, gazed
at the great father's house
and watched the river. And for a long time,

even years, you forgot about her.
Until you were about her age.

## Deliverance

Here's a story about a boy who hitchhiked to a little town to
locate a girl. He'd met her at a bus stop in his own town. In fact,
she'd missed her bus to drink a Coke with him, and had
to catch a later run. She'd seemed nervous, though alluring;
even mocking, though she'd just met him, as if
challenging him to do something about her, to claim her.
She'd written a phone number on the wrapper of a straw (like
some cabalistic code from her enigmatic other town), wadded it up
and flicked it at him, said he'd gotten her in trouble already
by making her miss the bus. "Thanks a lot," she'd said. Next day
he called the number. "No such folk here," said an old woman's
voice, irritated. So, he went to the road and stuck out his thumb.

He was picked up by a man whose head was a mass of tumors,
who'd grown his hair long to cover them, drove fast and carelessly
through the hilly country and laughed when the boy told him
where he was going and why. It was the first town he'd ever
arrived at by his own devices, so that—although it was only a
hamlet with a post office and boarded-up store—it seemed as
foreign as a village in Russia, exotic because a dying man drove him,
and absurd because he had no more information about the girl
than a wrong number and the name of her town.

Such stories finish only with the start of another—if we must have
endings. He later drove taxi in a run-down city—men to whore-
houses, hookers to bars, the Medicaid-sick to the doctor, and old
folks to bingo—and none of those stories have real endings. You see,
endings are larger illusions than the tales they are meant
to finish. In fact, once he swallowed a bottle of pills, and washed
it down with vodka to end everything but only awoke bewildered

in a hospital. And once his wife told him, "This is the *end,* you terrible man." But their lives went on together just the same, the same groceries, same dog, same I love yous. The same prayers at the end of the day for deliverance.

## Pennies

I used to find them on the sidewalk in a crooked trail,
like crumbs to lure a pigeon, all lying heads-up.
I swear, I thought my daughter was leaving me messages.
My shrink wore India print and sandals, and I was
a little in love with her. She shook her head. Delusions
are common with the grief-stricken, she said. She was
talking about the penny-messages, not the crush I had
on her. Hell, I knew crazy people make up half the earth,
and that I'd probably wandered to their side of the woods.
Yet I kept picking up the pennies. Eventually, they filled
a kitchen drawer, though the heads-up thing ended,
as it must. Such a run can't go indefinitely. And no more
trails, only random coppers. Now I believe three
heads in one day is lucky, while a preponderance
of tails-up means rejections, trouble at work, can't write,
can't think, and my students won't listen. Once I was
broke and sat all morning counting and rolling pennies
while a bead of sun slowly crossed my table. I spent them
on pumpernickel and salami; enough left over for cheap wine.
Crazy like a magpie, like a squirrel, crazy like a father.

## One Thing's for Sure

Mine's the first generation, or its sub-gen,
that faced the tube, Joe Friday, Red

Skelton, Jack Ruby, and saw no dream-difference
between them. I thought canned laughter

was people in other houses laughing at
the same shows.  But after fifty years of this stuff,

you can't fool a kid. The towers fall
and they know it's last season before the dust

is settled. You report live from an armored
convoy heading over the desert, talk to them

with tears like a father (which might be only
sand in your eyes), and it doesn't matter.

I woke up in my forties and found
myself childless. Is it too late? I asked.

Did they know I was an old rerun when
I walked into singles bars? Had they already

heard my jokes so many times; was everything
I knew on outdated software, inaccessible,

unviewable? One thing's for sure, I have to
stop this snorting about obsolescence. That's

death right there, you know.

## Daring to Call New York, 1978

Tonight you come in with snowy boots and pick
the farthest stool from the icy door, but it still doesn't
melt from your toes. You wish beer wasn't cold,
though you're not about to order it warm. The new bartender
is from New York City. He's shamed you into
drinking better beer, agitates you with talk
about places: the Village, Chelsea, and Lower East.

*I lived on Jones Street*, he told you once. *That's where
Dylan's walking with Suzie Rotolo on the cover
of* Blowin' in the Wind. *You ever get down there,
you ought to hit The White Horse Tavern where the poets drink,
or The Kettle of Fish where Dylan used to hang. Sure,
I knew Bobby back when he played the Village.
Nobody thought he'd amount to peanut shucks. But hey,
it could even happen to you. New York is like that.*

Tonight he's got another story: *I used to tend bar at a club
called Studio 12, where Caroline Kennedy goes every night.*
You say, No shit, you ever wait on her?
*Yeah, so what?* he says.
And twenty minutes later, when you've forgotten,
after he's pumped beer up and down the bar like
Communion in the Church of Disgruntlement, he suddenly
dumps a handful of change in front of you.
Says, *Go on, man, give the lady a call.*
You snort, Call who, my wife?
*No, stupid, Caroline.*
What the hell for?
*Why the hell not? You got somebody better to talk to?*

You guffaw and go to the phone at the end of the bar
where he can see you dropping coins.
*Two-dollars-and-eighty-five cents,*
*please-hold-for-the-number.* And now
you're causing a phone to ring far away
in a city so immense their garbage barges are bigger
than your miserable town;
you're making a jingling-sound
in the very heart of what's going down in New York.

A gravely voice says, *Studio 12.*
Yes...may I speak to...um, Caroline Kennedy, please?
The voice gets rougher, *Who's calling?*
You say, Tell her...this is Jim.

What a day. This morning you fell from a scaffold onto
a pile of rubble, and got only a scratch. You won
the check pool, too. And, though Sandy made
scrambled eggs for dinner, it's still been a day of lucky returns
on stupid endeavors (You'd been horsing on the scaffold,
and Sandy had made you swear not to gamble).

And now, someone's gone to fetch Caroline fuckin' Kennedy
for you. And yet, you wonder as you wait and drop more
quarters into the phone, why you can't explain
your own blues to yourself. This was a day when you swerved
for a white dog; and "When a Man Loves a Woman"
played  the instant you turned your ignition. Cool.
Yet, you *can't* explain these bastard blues. But, God,
dear God, please don't let me end up telling them to *her*!

## The Big Dipper

Three men are drinking, discussing
    the existence of God.
None can remember how they got
    on the subject, but odd

how it's held them like bugs in a
    flower, an hour or two
hours, more. Lolly, the step-child of
    one man, little girl, shrew,

appears at their table sudden-
    ly, her lower lip out
scolding him: *Mom's holding dinner,*
    she says, *don't rag her out*

*any longer.* She'd ridden her
    bike, so he stows it in
his trunk, jingles his keys. Lolly,
    sullen as a prison-

er, rides silent beside him.
    But there is always a
God when he drinks. He can always
    find the Spirit in a

spill on the table, in the sigh
    of his shoes on the sod.
Good God, bad God. He can pray as
    he drives, watching the od-

ometer turning his life like
   a log on a fire be-
cause he's had a few beers. His
   infernal thirst. And he

knows when that blood anemone
   deserts his veins, God too with-
draws again like floodwater, he's
   dead naked. Only myth-

ology has given us men
   as lonely as he, O-
dysseus,  or Job, yes that poor
   dumb bastard Job—although

what drinking man can't imagine
   himself covered with boils
while his wife curses him. Drinking
   too is more damned toil

than it could ever be worth if
   not for its illumin-
ation of the world, the singing,
   the vivid illumin-

ation of his own path, even
   unto this very mo-
ment in which he's driving his wife's
   sullen daughter (and no

one knows his love for this half-
    orphan) home to dinner
while his blood anemone fades—
    no hosannas, sinner—

the darkling fields becoming
    more akin to the in-
finite cold that stretches between
    stars, between Orion

the hunter, say, and the Dipper,
    that damned-thirsty Dipper.

*Mirrors*

What is it about mirrors that some
folks cover them after a death
in the house? They're removed
from the baths of zen centers
during silent retreats as if they
made clamor, complained, told jokes.

Of all animals only monkeys and humans
know themselves in a mirror. Only
humans give a damn, bargain with it,
practice themselves. Yet, how calmly
it replies, *You*, while you wash
the night's hell from your mouth.

It says more to your lover, and kinder.
*What?* you snort. *Put a mirror over my bed?*
*I'd wake and think my soul was escaping.*

All right, the mirror is not your friend,
not as symbol, metaphor, or actual fact.
You might even cover the importunate thing
if you're sure it won't cost your life.

## Fearful Symmetry

> *Did he who made the lamb make thee?*
> —William Blake

I remember thinking it would all
      work— lambs we were, thinking
        we deserved what

we dreamed: our clothes in a pile
      beside a bed in a house
        that we never

actually acquired.  But I won't
      bother detailing the
        troubles of mixed-

color lovers thirty-seven years ago
      (*stars throw down their spears*,
        hell, you better

believe, & forget it). Except for
      one incident, one night
        making love

in my car on the black wooded
      reservation road, when
        a car load of

boozy towners halted & jumped
      on my hood, on my roof,
        then attempted to

tip us over. Terrified at
      the wheel I floored it, I
            spun, I raced

crazy naked across the res,
      she screaming under the
            blanket. But *shit,*

nothing to say    after all but
      *shit.* Except that as I
            was spinning my

tires in that gravel trying to
      get the hell gone, my eyes
            near those eyes

in my side window, I swear I saw
      my own fire-face burning,
            in a fearful

symmetry, heart-breakingly hungry,
      trying to open the door
            to devour us.

## For My 19,723$^{rd}$ Day (My 54$^{th}$ Birthday)

Why do we pretend every year there's one day
that's different? As if your ass is any lighter
on that day. But you know you'd better party,
drink that magnum of merlot, only later to go
over a roaring fall of sadness like Bogart in his boat,
his gin bottles floating behind in the river.

Speaking of movies, you think yours is endless
for the first god-knows-how-many-thousand days,
then you realize you're probably on the last reel.
You've got more daring escapes to do, but you
won't get the girl. It's one of *those* movies.

Three

# Travail

Seesaw, Margery Daw,
Jacky shall have a new master;
Jacky shall have but a penny a day,
Because he can work no faster.
—Anonymous

*work out your own salvation with fear and trembling.*
—Paul to the Phillipians 2:12

*Travail*

1. *What's the most wonderful machine*

*you've ever seen?* the teacher asked.
The answer she wanted was the human body.
But one kid said, *An ice-block cutter*
*I saw down in Georgia.* The lesson didn't inspire us
        to be machines,
busted before we're paid for. Everything breaks:
        that familiar grind of gears,
the melancholy stink when a resister burns,
another gadget kicked across the floor,
        piece of crap going back
to the store, wonderful though it was.
But we, swell little bastards of *duck 'n' cover*,
        deliver us from brokenness.

2. *Future Farmers*

The best boys were called to buck hay till
age seventy-five, to castrate a steer
& rescue a breach-birth calf
   under a dusty bulb,
to father eight or ten daughters & whip sense
into their heads (their character would be
their dowry) & one smoking bull of a son,
   inhale a cyclone
   & vote for Nixon.
Corn & cabbage piled to the moon. All stuff
you'll never do; if you started now
   you'd never learn in time
to save yourself, the moon would be gone
for good before you'd built much of a pile.
You failed shit-shoveling, got a C in
   chicken whacking.
   So get out, get out,
leave before the bringing of the sheaves,
   or everyone's rejoicing
will break you. Slip like a piglet under the gate.
Life is a joke. I mean, it's obvious,
   if only to you.

3. *The Cutter*

A Yankee boy visiting Georgia, I'd just
used the colored shit house; dumb
creature of curiosity when I  came out.
A white man dollied a pillar of ice
across a cold-house floor & tripped it
        into a steel cage
inside which it tumbled of its own weight
        end over end
like an acrobat through a gauntlet of knives
split-ting & flipping & split-ting again,
        skid-ding out
the other end in ten-pound blocks
        (you could lick).
The paint was worn off the magic cage,
        its knives sharpened
a thousand & fifty times down to wavy, lurid grins
        that caught your breath.
Men stood around sweating & smoking
        & looking at it.
Didn't matter they'd seen it before.

4. *The Chain*

Earth is a banquet. Ants feed on a dog turd,
lugging it in pieces back to their hill,
dog steals the brie from my table when
     my head is turned,
love beckons over candles (the cosmic
bribe of reproduction), & from
five thousand miles came this cabernet.
     Intelligence isn't
just knowledge, they say; *real* brains
(not just beating me at chess, or finishing
the crossword in four minutes) is the
ability to connect seemingly
     disparate things:
the work of the ants on a turd in
New York, to lovers drinking wine,
     to the money they spent,
the bull-work of the French farmer,
then figure in the French & American
     Revolutions,
hillside vineyard temperature,   phases
     of   the   moon,
the bacteria in the farmer's soil,
the unalienable claim of worms.
     There's a chain
in there somewhere, linking all things,
for a smarter & soberer man  than me.

5. *Night*

At 3 AM I drove past that damned shirt factory
(where I had to be in a few
hours), bag with a bottle of
        wine I'd worked
like a dog to earn, just enough gas
to get home if I didn't idle the
        engine too long
while pissing by the road, while thinking
what a tired turd I'd become,
        on the same back road
        where Captain Morgan
was hung by those businessmen-kidnappers
        back in 1826
for giving away the Masons' secrets,
        & dumped
in a hole for the worms & ants. Life is
        a banquet.
        There's a chain
there somewhere, I can feel it snaking around
my leg, but I'm afraid to look.

6. *Hercules*

My thirteenth labor was to swallow my own
bitter hump: How little good  ever came of my work.
        You laugh, but imagine
who lived downstream of the Augean stables.
Or the golden girdle I swiped from
Hippolyte (whatever the poets claim,
        it was an undergarment,
I took it off her myself) which carried lice
to the daughter of King Eurystheus.
Then the three-headed rat-faced dog I captured
in hell, just so the King could free him
        meaner than ever.
A few golden apples (whatever the poets say)
aren't worth a year of your life. But enough
about me. You, Jack Shit, or whatever
your name is, wake up every day
        & sit on your bedside,
have your coffee before you do
        your Hercules thing, meet
        that quota, catch
that boar on the mountain, kill the Hydra,
        swipe that account
from your biggest competitor, & buck 'n' bronco
that flesh-eating horse into submission.
While the king dreams up twelve labors more,
you swallow that hump I left
        on the table for you.

## 7. *Meanwhile*

*I got me a deal*, said the old
        black man cutting
cabbage. *I work by the hour*, he said,
*I don't do no piece work,*
        *no suh.*
The fat guys running the farm
let him go on believing,
        meanwhile
        counting
his bushels of cabbage,
while he knelt, aching his red-
eyed way down the row.
        Meanwhile
the rest of us humped it hard
till we dropped. Then I grumped:
        I'd had enough.
*Screw it*, I said, & walked away.
I was the only college boy.

8. *My Father, Rowing*

Interns & nurses laugh
outside my father's door, & pinch
each other's asses.  This must be
the hell I've always
heard about, that he warned
would come due:  not to him,
he'd meant, but to me if I didn't
do     say the right     didn't put,
look proper     man the oars
learn where
            the windows
of heaven unlatch. Yet, yet, yet
here *he* lies, tired arms of a rivet
pounder, brittle as corn.

I have his nose & his chin
& sundry. Just like mine, his boat
always fills up with bilge
before he rows very far.
But like me he *rows*. Neither
of us are lucky warts. But now when
he dips his oars there's no shore,
            but fog bank,
some buoy with a dumbfounding
code, some overlapping dream. So, so, so—
will I be rewarded some day
with the same shorted-out
wires? Like a phone that rings

but won't talk sense?—
    *Ha, I got old*
    *& my head got*
*on the wrong boat, ha ha—*
    I hate myself
for wondering thus, at a time
like this. A man worked hard,
his wife worked damned hard to
get to this room. A man came home
from work ten thousand nights
    wondering, even
then, where he was really rowing.

9. *The Rhythms*
> *Love your rhythm and give rhythm to your actions*
> *under its law, as well as to your verses*
> —Rubén Darío

I grew up knowing & believing
      the incessant rhythm:
work / work / work / *break*
kettle-drumming through my life,
boom / boom / boom / *phew-w!*
or actually, applied to a seven-day
      measure
        it's five spondees: / / / / /
for Monday through Friday
& two unstressed measures – –
like a fusillade of *damns*
followed by two orgasmic *ahhh*s,
      & *selah*, & *selah*,


& so on, depending on how much
you cherish your weekends, your
down time, your ear for
your own heartbeat & breath.
      In earlier times,
before we thought leisure important,
      factories still ran on
      Genesis schedule:
*six* mornings in a row up & out
the door like God with a world
      under construction.

But, most Americans working
now don't recall the most punitive labor.
They read *The Jungle* in college
& tried to forget it. Because
        this beat,
this *omni* rhythm, comes not from
scripture, not from law, but
        up from the earth
itself, booming its rightness
into our bones, noses, sinuses, bowels.
Somehow even thrumming
        with the blue
PULSE in my wrist. Until *somehow*

a half-beat extra ticked its way in
(I hardly noticed), like a mole; like
a doctor will listen to your chest
& say, You've got an extra beat
going, Charlie. He'll order a battery
of tests. But no one explores
        the real source
        of this free radical,
new spondee, this renegade stress that's
        punctured my rhythm. Though
of course it's born of office crises
        which seemed—though
I can't say why—to echo upsets at
home, as the torrential weather in *Lear* mirrored
the king's ruined house.  So, an extra
        Saturday morning

at the office soon
became limitless, back to Genesis 1 & 2,
& worse. Forget the clock & the calendar—
& forget the rhythm,
& whack your brother
& take your mark,
these new stresses, these booms now go
on in my sleep.
But I hate to complain, or even
bring it up. Complaining does not
become me.

10: *Businessman Without a Cause*

This was about as close to real as a dream ever gets.
I mean, we were *there*, Harris & me,
sitting at our desks on that dark field,
              side by side,
our associates standing about.
First we practiced rolling out of our
              chairs & hopping
back to our feet, straightening our ties,
grass stains on our sleeves.
              I had no pants
because it was a dream, but no one
paid any mind except to our impending
              chicken race.


We revved our terminals, & our desks
trembled & shimmied. Harris flashed that
              *gotcha* grin he'd given me
a thousand times in meetings when
              he'd knifed my back.
At the pom-pom signal from Office-
              Manager Alice I pointed
& clicked *GO* & slammed the RETURN key.
We burst out of our cubicles, two desks racing
              over the lumpy ground
              toward the precipice
& that very void I'd warned everyone
a million times was out there waiting, gaping—
which no one ever disputed, but now I saw

*it* had *become,*
or rather, *it had always been* THE GAME.
My drawers rattled, my coffee cup
flew over my shoulder, graphs
              popped on my screen—
pies & bars, soaring statistical reds
& greens: how close, how *close* was the edge?
(Check Dow, check Standard & quick dump
              all those Congo mines,
                   sell Proctor & Kodak &—)—


*Harris rolled out of his chair! Ha!* He
              panicked first!
tumbling over the ground like a
              road-kill rabbit.
I yelled, "So long, you chicken-shit bastard!"
But then at the edge, when I tried
              to bale out myself,
I'd caught my thing in my center drawer,
& a splittance later my desk dragged me
              dick & all,
over the edge. But you don't hit bottom


in dreams. I woke the whole house screaming.
I got up & sat on the edge of my bed.
"Go back to sleep," I told my wife.
              "Go to sleep everyone."
I soaked my face in the cold sink,
              & dressed for work.

Four

# Alabaster

*Boarding a Bus*


In a small-knit Iowa town I watched
a couple board the bus and take the seat
behind me. They'd waited till then to count
their cash. I could hear each of them whisper
fives and ones like vespers, and repeat, then declare
they couldn't afford to go. "But," she added,
"we haven't had a vacation in—" "That's
very true," he said. And they sighed into the rolling scene:
the sunset on a sea of corn,
a lonely red gas station, an old man changing a flat.
I don't want to scare anyone, but
this is your life too. Tell me how it's any different.

## Alabaster

*—Batavia, New York*

We didn't know who'd lived in the apartment
before us, only that they'd gone and left
the dingy furniture. Dolly the landlady
tromped up the stairs on the first
of each month demanding cash flat in her hand,
as if she'd just woke from
a nightmare that Buzak and I had skipped out on her.

Once when he swept the floor, Buzak found
two purple pills in a crack in the wood.
We studied them, and held them
in our palms, tiny hexagons,
and scratched them with our thumbnails.
Cops parked across the street, watching our
windows, apparently thinking we

were those same guys, the ones who'd fled, who
not long ago had dreamed in our beds,
who'd left (in addition to the furniture) a tomato,
half a beer, and protein powder in the fridge,
a footprint on my bedroom ceiling, and an unmailed letter
to someone named *Slake*, pleading
for time. Just time.
As if Slake governed the rotation of the planet.

When the cops burst through the downstairs door
they stomped on the stairs like drunken monkeys
in the service of bedlam, banged on a door—
"Open up! Police!"—
and took a man across the hall away.
We let our breath out like tired balloons.

But the next day the cops were across the street
again, watching. I was afraid to take
a shower: imagined officers leading me naked
and dripping to a patrol car
at the curb. Finally afraid to come home from work at all.

One summer night Buzak got the purple
pills out. We held them in our palms again.
Hexagons. Tiny talismans.
Sitting at the window we washed them down
with jasmine tea.
And watched the city turn to alabaster.

## Cleaning Your Skillet

A little vinegar cuts most of the grit. Then rubbing with salt breaks the last
kernels of a charred dinner long ago for old friends (now vanished or who
even betrayed you, whoever they were, before me anyway), some burnt sauté
of beef, or maybe sesame oil and onion forgotten on the fire while you
slipped to the dining room where the placenta of some rumor was being
buried among you, until a sudden nosegay of smoke—that same primal
alarm that frightens bees back to their hives to grab all the honey they can
carry. But now: vinegar, salt, and a finishing coat of olive oil— listen, it
gongs clean, clear and empty.

## What My Cats Know

They know the earth is small, flat, bordered on all sides
by bungalows. In the winter when I come in, this house is

suddenly warmer, or cooler in the summer, unaccountably.
I bring light when I arrive in the dark. And I have

more sorcery: a laser pen light, a microwave pet-bed warmer.
This is how religions get started, except that I'm getting older,

I've had surgeries and I'm putting on weight and I cry a lot.
It's all covered, of course: the doctor visits and the blood work

and medication that makes my balancing act of moods
possible. In fact, these pills make me not give enough

of a damn. I've got the laser out and I'm terrorizing
my cats. This is the way ignorance gets started.

People think it starts at the bottom. It doesn't.

## The Facts

Somewhere you read that ants make up
ten-to-fifteen percent of earth's animal
mass. You probably heard it on some
*Nova* episode or the Animal Channel.
You're fascinated by this factoid, dumb-
founded almost. God, maybe there's more
ants than human- and cattle-mass combined,
even throwing in worms, beetles
and birds. But, unfortunately, your head
has been chock-full lately, and this
ant fact is one fact too many, doomed
to leave your head by 10 PM like Cleveland-
bound passengers, like so many facts
before it that found no hospitality in your skull,
that joined the great dark sum of knowledge
you were offered but couldn't retain.

—You suspect that, since your fiftieth
birthday, more facts are departing your
head than arriving, although they hit
like a storm, facts whizzing by like barcodes
on Conrail cars, and the damned train
is an endless chug toward extinction.
*The human condition*, you think with a shrug,
*the natural way of the universe: oblivion.*
Even while you ponder, galaxies are
flying farther apart, thus making
more darkness between them. And
that is just more ignorant space.

—Are you still with me on this? Because
the worst thing is that darkness comes to
claim us eventually. It invades your house
just at bedtime—not *ordinary* dark, the half-
lighted stuff we have in the city, but the real,
pure, soul-sucking unknown, the tar flood
of ignorance seeping under your door
and filling your kitchen and dining room.

—Only knowledge fends it back. You've
got to reorganize that head and make more
room for your intelligence, more facts,
because that dark flood is now up to your
knees. You dash upstairs and speed-read
a couple books; call Information Please,
listen to Berlitz tapes on fast-forward,
call the Bertrand Russell Society and get
them out of bed— "Quick, explain Spinoza,"
you holler to them. "Give me Erasmus
and Bacon." Until the dark is appeased
somewhat, receding by inches. "Please,"
you beg into the phone, "tell me what
Plato knew." And, finally the flood retreats.

—When your mother visits on Sunday,
you show her the high darkness mark
on your wall. Shaking her head she
says, "You never were a listener. It'll
come back if you don't pay attention."

—And it does. The dark comes conquering
again. It needs no prince to lead it, but
comes of its own urgency, fluid and black
and famished into your yard, over
your welcome mat, into your house,
and up your stairs. You grab Herodotus'
*Histories*, do frantic and random Google
searches. Jump from Aquinas to Kant to
Heidegger. Once again you're on the phone—
to whom? Your high school teachers are
dead now. Your college professors
are retired and gone from the phone book.
They're probably losing their memories
too, and couldn't help you anyway.

—Then you notice: The idiot next door
is watching TV, having a Budweiser,
dry and bright as an oasis in Egypt.

## With Some Poets in Baltimore, 2003

Only now in America could such a harbor
be empty of ships, save
one moored permanently
and lighted for tourists, for our tips.
We walk by the water until the snow becomes heavy;
the poets are the ones who
come in from the weather
and drink in the bar, others out walking
are homeless. All of us
have lost loves, some lost families;
but the worst losses even poets are unable to name.
Our fingers push money across the bar.
The seafood is from somewhere else,
not from this water, and never will be.
Some stay here forever and wait, some move
inland and try their luck. Others
simply wonder why things continue.
Look, the president is on the TV above the lobby
like a talking clock. You look
at your watch—you want to dispute the time.
And there's always more news,
isn't there? A rumor of war
means there is a war. There's always
more harbor, rumor of harbor, always more darkness.

## A Likely Story, Actaeon

There was no woman in that water, much less
a goddess. Your stag face and horns are

yourself turned inside out, perhaps because
you want too much. Yes, it can happen, these

ugly transformations. I knew a barber turned monkey,
and a professor of law gone muskrat. A multi-

fauna lycanthropy has been going on as long
as anyone knows: without warning your inner

beast asserts. It could happen to the president:
making a speech denouncing the natural world
as the enemy, suddenly an anteater stands

before the press. Circe understood this, she
needed no sorcery: throw a party and men

will be pigs. Scientists are working on this,
Actaeon. But they're human too, and barely

holding themselves together. It doesn't take
a goddess to ruin you. That's all I'm saying.

## That Was When We Got Lost, after the Movie

driving for home in the dark.
We were in love, and love removes

uneasiness about where you're going. You're
glad to be lost, even knowing hindsight is ahead.

But what we saw in our windshield was
a coat dragging behind a car, and we

didn't even ask if we should follow,
because in the movie a man had been dragged

behind a horse, hanging on hard,
and he was in love. Well, I'll tell you who it was:

Clark Gable. Later his wife would
blame John Huston for causing his fatal heart attack,

and Marilyn would die too.
And us? We just went on following that coat,

empty of a body, driven by we never knew who.

*Short Wave Radio*


Beyond those green digits and decimals
     an aviary of voices:
          Radio Moscow,

Thunder Bay, and all those wild tongues
     like a furious counting of
          marbles. Say *Moga- moga-*

*Mogadishu* a hundred times fast. How
     bad you wanted to be lost
          in the farness

of dialects that crackled and whistled as your
     boy-hand twisted the knob across
          the Steppes, the Pampas,

over the dusty Gobi. And Nairobi! One day
     you dreamed past your school bus stop
          and rode it in black rain

all the way to a dark garage where the
     mechanics found you, lunch pail
          on your lap.

Then an overhead fan film-noired the shadows
     around a man in khaki at a desk
          who smoked and spoke

to a radio mic: *We got a kid here, Mort* [crackle-
squawwwk]. *His mother's gotta be
tearin' her hair.*

[ptttttt-fwheeeee-crackle] *He wants to know
if he's in Africa. Yeah, that's
what I said, Africa.*

How you hated the dreary nexus of clotheslines
across the neighborhood, and those
crabapple scrub-lots,

though they hid exotic spiders, reputedly
deadly, that had stowed north
on banana boats,

and though  those ugly lots were also mafia
dumping grounds, and though your
city's name—Buffalo—

would likely fool some other kid with a radio
into thinking it wild and western,
you knew too well

the reek of steel mills, and domestic gray;
and you knew from long listening
that no place,

no one place would ever be world enough.

## Nothing Holds Up Like Your Bones

Mine are still axel-hard in my fifties. My hair,
meanwhile, grows for harvest. Skin molts,
muscles soften like a bicycle tire over winter.
My heart is an oft-regenerated collection of fibers,
not the same that addled my brain in love.
Even my personality I've modified for
the comfort of others. But my bones,
my dear skeleton, never stand aloof from me,
nor look in the mirror, yet they subtly
convince me I'm here, even when my own
reflection makes me doubtful. Old bones,
the last crumple of junk to be ascribed
my name, I celebrate you now while there's
still time. I rub you like a dog in gratitude.

## The Oregon Poet at the Grange Hall

After someone screws in a fuse the lights
come on again, weak juice from old arteries
behind the plaster walls. The Oregon poet stands up,
pulls a wad of poems out of his sweater pocket.
Then someone plugs in the coffee pot
and the lights go out again. It's raining too.
I wondered if my old Plymouth would
get me here. It's not like I take good care of it
and have any reasonable expectations.
Mother instilled the notion of consequences in
her children, and I was her honor pupil.
But I made it here, while the horizon glared
that greenish light that usually means a storm
for the record books. No storm, however.
Only rain, and the gargling downspouts.
The lights come on again, and the Oregon poet
stands up. Bill is nothing if not a patient man,
can pick up where he left off, or not.
Then someone plugs in the coffee.

—*For William Stafford 1914–1993*

## Left on the Road in the Nevada Desert

This happened so long ago it seems like someone else's story,
a braver person, stronger than me.

Because I didn't care much that I was stranded there
with only a couple swallows of water, heat building in the silence.

What mattered was the small truck that passed.
Half a mile beyond, it turned off the highway. I watched it

for a long time, traveling a dirt road toward the mountains,
morning glittering on its roof,

a thin wake of dust hanging in its path without settling,
which made me think I'll never die.

## Sleeping on the Mountain

*But be ye satisfied that you have light*
*Enough to take your step and find your foothold . . .*
—T. S. Eliot, "The Rock"

I slept in my car last night, baby, along
a mountain road up north in Vermont
under black shoulders of granite,
the sucking undertow of passing trucks
rocking me like a rowboat while I slipped
into nothing like the moon disappearing
in the trees. Once, years ago, I was
driving somewhere late and drooping
and pulled over to sleep, and in the morning
found myself in a strange town fifty
miles or more off course. Another
time I fell asleep while pulling into my
parking space at home and bashed my
head against the windshield. But this time,
this life, this night was different, baby:
you and I have shared all the pale adjectives
of loneliness, and gone beyond
them like slow cars, and so, satisfied that
I have moon enough to find my step
and foothold, why should I push the mountain?
I stopped to sleep before I had to. Yes, I'm
smarter now. I walked down a lane to water
the fog-laden ferns, then took my pills
before curling up in my old yoga blanket.
Half-way up the mountain, as I mean to say.

*Bless*


the gang kid who let me escape, told me to run down
an alley, *Get lost, get lost*
and probably had to invent a story when
the bigger bully wanted to know where their
prisoner went; bless
my grandmother who didn't tell my father
so many times it would
fill the Book of Acts, probably
thinking whatever I'd done wasn't worth the belt

and God was watching anyway;
bless the couple who picked me up in the desert
and drove me fast
to an Orange Crush machine;
all the bartenders who served me under-age
in apparent innocence;
the cops who let me go for speeding because it was late

and they wanted to go home themselves,
*Plus the kid's only half a mile from his driveway;*
and the other cops who confiscated
my razors and kitchen knives
on the worst afternoon of my life;
the bar maid in Pittsburgh who gave me a bourbon
and sandwich after hours when
my blood sugar had dropped like a load of scrap.
Ah, miracle workers.

"Attica." In the first day of an uprising at the Attica Correctional Facility, Attica, NY, September 9, 1971, one guard was mortally wounded at the hands of inmates. Hostages were taken, and a standoff began that lasted until the morning of September 13, when Governor Rockefeller ordered state police to retake the prison. All the rest of the thirty-nine deaths (both guards and inmates) were by police bullets on that last day. The public was particularly frightened by television and newspaper images of the hoods worn by prisoners to protect their identities from the media. The foundry referred to in the poem was the Westinghouse facility in the Village of Attica, now closed.

"Fearful Symmetry." The reservation referred to is the Tonawanda reservation of Senecas in Western New York.

"Night." Capt. William Morgan, of Batavia, NY, wrote a book in 1826 exposing secrets of the Masonic Order. He published it locally, and shortly thereafter was kidnapped and probably murdered, although no one was charged with the crime. A body was found in Lake Ontario, more than fifty miles away, and a coroner's inquest ruled that it was Morgan, and death by drowning. Many historians doubt that the body was, in fact, Morgan. Nevertheless, the scandal resulting from the disappearance had far-reaching political consequences, turning public sentiment against the Masons nationwide.

"Businessman Without a Cause." This last section of the poem "Travail" is, in part, a parody of the 1955 movie *Rebel Without a Cause* in which James Dean drives in a fatal chicken race toward the edge of a cliff.

Steven Huff grew up in rural Western New York, worked as a taxi driver, foundry man, and reporter, and later as an editor-publisher with BOA Editions, Ltd. He now teaches writing at Rochester Institute of Technology and at the Eastman School of Music, and has a weekly radio show, "Fiction in Shorts," on NPR-affiliate stations, WXXI-FM, and WJSL-FM. His first book of poems, *The Water We Came From*, was published in 2003. A collection of stories, *A Pig in Paris*, is due out in 2007. He lives in Rochester, NY.